OF
—

By

SAROJINI NAIDU

WITH AN
INTRODUCTION
BY EDMUND GOSSE

CONTENTS

4

INTRODUCTION

It is only at the request, that is to say at the command, of a dear and valued friend that I consent to write these few sentences. It would seem that an "introduction" can only be needed when the personage to be "introduced" is unknown in a world prepared to welcome her but still ignorant of her qualities. This is certainly not the case with Mrs. Naidu, whose successive volumes, of which this is the third, have been received in Europe with approval, and in India with acclamation. Mrs. Naidu is, I believe, acknowledged to be the most accomplished living poet of India—at least, of those who write in English, since what lyric wonders the native languages of that country may be producing I am not competent to say. But I do not think that any one questions the supreme place she holds among those Indians who choose to write in our tongue. Indeed, I am not disinclined to believe that she is the most brilliant, the most original, as well as the most correct, of all the natives of Hindustan who have written in English. And I say this without prejudice to the fame of that delicious Toru Dutt, so exquisite in her fragility, whose life and poems it was my privilege to reveal to the world thirty years ago. For in the case of Toru Dutt, beautiful as her writings were, there was much in them to be excused by her youth, her solitude, the extremely pathetic circumstances of her brief and melancholy career. In the maturer work of Mrs. Naidu I find nothing, or almost nothing, which the severest criticism could call in question.

In a gracious sentence, published seven or eight years ago, Sarojini Naidu declared that it was the writer of this preface "who first showed" her "the way to the golden threshold" of poetry. This is her generous mode of describing certain conditions which I may perhaps be allowed to enlarge upon so far as they throw light on the contents of the volume before us. It is needless for me to repeat those particulars of the Indian poet's early life, so picturesque and so remarkable, which were given by Mr. Arthur Symons in the excellent essay which he prefixed to her volume of *1905*. Sufficient for my purpose it is to say that when Sarojini Chattopddhyay—as she then was—first made her appearance in London, she was a child of sixteen years, but as unlike the usual English maiden of that age as a lotus or a cactus is unlike a lily of the valley. She was already marvellous in mental maturity, amazingly well read, and far beyond a Western child in all her acquaintance with the world.

By some accident—now forgotten, but an accident most fortunate for us—Sarojini was introduced to our house at an early date after her arrival in London, and she soon became one of the most welcome and intimate of our guests. It was natural that one so impetuous and so sympathetic should not long conceal from her hosts the fact that she was writing copiously in verse— in English verse. I entreated to be allowed to see what she had composed, and a bundle of MSS. was slipped into my hand. I hastened to examine it as soon as I was alone, but now there followed a disappointment, and with it an embarrassment, which, in the face of what followed, I make no scruple of revealing. The verses which Sarojini had entrusted to me were skilful in form, correct in grammar and blameless in sentiment, but they had the disadvantage of being totally without individuality. They were Western in feeling and in imagery; they were founded on reminiscences of Tennyson and Shelley; I am not sure that they did not even breathe an atmosphere of Christian resignation.

I laid them down in despair; this was but the note of the mocking-bird with a vengeance.

It was not pleasant to daunt the charming and precocious singer by so discouraging a judgment; but I reflected on her youth and her enthusiasm, and I ventured to speak to her sincerely. I advised the consignment of all that she had written, in this falsely English vein, to the waste-paper basket. I implored her to consider that from a young Indian of extreme sensibility, who had mastered not merely the language but the prosody of the West, what we wished to receive was, not a réchauffé of Anglo-Saxon sentiment in an Anglo-Saxon setting, but some revelation of the heart of India, some sincere penetrating analysis of native passion, of the principles of antique religion and of such mysterious intimations as stirred the soul of the East long before the West had begun to dream that it had a soul. Moreover, I entreated Sarojini to write no more about robins and skylarks, in a landscape of our Midland counties, with the village bells somewhere in the distance calling the parishioners to church, but to describe the flowers, the fruits, the trees, to set her poems firmly among the mountains, the gardens, the temples, to introduce to us the vivid populations of her own voluptuous and unfamiliar province; in other words, to be a genuine Indian poet of the Deccan, not a clever machine-made imitator of the English classics.

With the docility and the rapid appreciation of genius, Sarojini instantly accepted and with as little delay as possible acted upon this suggestion. Since *1895* she has written, I believe, no copy of verses which endeavours to conceal the exclusively Indian source of her inspiration, and she indulges with too enthusiastic gratitude the friend whose only merit was to show her "the way to the golden threshold." It has been in her earlier collections, and it will be found to be in this, the characteristic of Mrs. Naidu's writing that she is in all things and to the fullest extent autochthonous. She springs from the very soil of India; her spirit, although it employs the English language as its vehicle, has no other tie with the West.

It addresses itself to the exposition of emotions which are tropical and primitive, and in this respect, as I believe, if the poems of Sarojini Naidu be carefully and delicately studied they will be found as luminous in lighting up the dark places of the East as any contribution of savant or historian. They have the astonishing advantage of approaching the task of interpretation from inside the magic circle, although armed with a technical skill that has been cultivated with devotion outside of it.

Those who have enjoyed the earlier collections of Mrs. Naidu's poems will find that in "The Bird of Time" the note of girlish ecstasy has passed, and that a graver music has taken its place. She has lived—and this is another facet of her eminent career—in close companionship with sorrow; she has known the joy and also the despair of consolation. The sight of much suffering, it may be, has thinned her jasmine-garlands and darkened the azure of her sky. It is known to the world that her labours for the public weal have not been carried out without deep injury to her private health. But these things have not slackened the lyric energy of Sarojini; they have rather given it intensity. She is supported, as the true poet must be, by a noble ambition. In her childhood she dreamed magnificently; she hoped to be a Goethe or a Keats for India. This desire, like so many others, may prove too heavy a strain for a heart that

"s'ouvrit comme une fleur profonde
Dont l'auguste corolle a prédit l'orient."

But the desire for beauty and fame, the magnificent impulse, are still energetic within this burning soul.

These few words I venture to bring to a close with a couple of sentences from one of her own latest letters: "While I live, it will always be the supreme desire of my Soul to write poetry—one poem, one line of enduring verse even. Perhaps I shall die without realising that longing which is at once an exquisite joy and an unspeakable anguish to me." The reader of "The Bird of Time" will feel satisfied that this her sad apprehension is needless.

EDMUND GOSSE

SONGS
OF NATURE

TO MY
FAIRY FANCIES

———————

NAY, no longer I may hold you,
　　In my spirit's soft caresses,
Nor like lotus-leaves enfold you
　　In the tangles of my tresses.
Fairy fancies, fly away
　　To the white cloud-wildernesses,
　　　　Fly away!

Nay, no longer ye may linger
　　With your laughter-lighted faces,
Now I am a thought-worn singer
　　In life's high and lonely places.
Fairy fancies, fly away,
　　To bright wind-inwoven spaces,
　　　　Fly away!

LEILI

THE serpents are asleep among the poppies,
The fireflies light the soundless panther's way
To tangled paths where shy gazelles are straying,
And parrot-plumes outshine the dying day.
O soft! the lotus-buds upon the stream
Are stirring like sweet maidens when they dream.

A caste-mark on the azure brows of Heaven,
The golden moon burns sacred, solemn, bright
The winds are dancing in the forest-temple,
And swooning at the holy feet of Night.
Hush! in the silence mystic voices sing
And make the gods their incense-offering.

IN THE FOREST

———

HERE, O my heart, let us burn the dear dreams that
    are dead,
Here in this wood let us fashion a funeral pyre
Of fallen white petals and leaves that are mellow and
    red,
Here let us burn them in noon's flaming torches of fire.

We are weary, my heart, we are weary, so long we have
    borne
The heavy loved burden of dreams that are dead, let us
    rest,
Let us scatter their ashes away, for a while let us
    mourn;
We will rest, O my heart, till the shadows are gray in
    the west.

But soon we must rise, O my heart, we must wander
　　again
Into the war of the world and the strife of the throng;
Let us rise, O my heart, let us gather the dreams that
　　remain,
We will conquer the sorrow of life with the sorrow of
　　song.

IN A
TIME OF FLOWERS

O LOVE! do you know the spring is here
With the lure of her magic flute? . . .
The old earth breaks into passionate bloom
At the kiss of her fleet, gay foot.
The burgeoning leaves on the almond boughs,
And the leaves on the blue wave's breast
Are crowned with the limpid and delicate light
Of the gems in your turban-crest.
The bright pomegranate buds unfold,
The frail wild lilies appear,
Like the blood-red jewels you used to fling
O'er the maidens that danced at the feast of spring
To welcome the new-born year.

O Love! do you know the spring is here? . . .
The dawn and the dusk grow rife
With scent and song and tremulous mirth,
The blind, rich travail of life.

The winds are drunk with the odorous breath
Of *henna*, *sarisha*, and *neem* . . .
Do they ruffle your cold, strange, tranquil sleep,
Or trouble your changeless dream
With poignant thoughts of the world you loved,
And the beauty you held so dear?
Do you long for a brief, glad hour to wake
From your lonely slumber for sweet love's sake,
To welcome the new-born year?

NASTURTIUMS

POIGNANT and subtle and bitter perfume,
Exquisite, luminous, passionate bloom,
Your leaves interwoven of fragrance and fire
Are Savitri's sorrow and Sita's desire,
Draupadi's longing, Damayanti's fears,
And sweetest Sakuntala's magical tears.

These ore the immortal women of Sanscrit legend
and song, whose poignant sorrows and radiant virtues
still break the heart and inspire the lives of Indian
women.

GOLDEN CASSIA

O BRILLIANT blossoms that strew my way,
You are only woodland flowers they say.

But, I sometimes think that perchance you are
Fragments of some new-fallen star;

Or golden lamps for a fairy shrine,
Or golden pitchers for fairy wine.

Perchance you are, O frail and sweet!
Bright anklet-bells from the wild spring's feet,

Or the gleaming tears that some fair bride shed
Remembering her lost maidenhead.

But now, in the memoried dusk you seem
The glimmering ghosts of a bygone dream.

CHAMPAK BLOSSOMS

AMBER petals, ivory petals,
Petals of carven jade,
Charming with your ambrosial sweetness
Forest and field and glade,
Foredoomed in your hour of transient glory
To shrivel and shrink and fade!

Tho' mango blossoms have long since vanished,
And orange blossoms be shed,
They live anew in the luscious harvests
Of ripening yellow and red;
But you, when your delicate bloom is over,
Will reckon amongst the dead.

Only to girdle a girl's dark tresses
Your fragrant hearts are uncurled:
Only to garland the vernal breezes
Your fragile stars are unfurled.
You make no boast in your purposeless beauty
To serve or profit the world.

Yet, 'tis of you thro' the moonlit ages
That maidens and minstrels sing,
And lay your buds on the great god's altar,
O radiant blossoms that fling
Your rich, voluptuous, magical perfume
To ravish the winds of spring.

ECSTASY

HEART, O my heart! lo, the springtime is waking
      In meadow and grove.
Lo, the mellifluous *koels* are making
      Their paeans of love.
Behold the bright rivers and rills in their glancing,
      Melodious flight,
Behold how the sumptuous peacocks are dancing
      In rhythmic delight.

Shall we in the midst of life's exquisite chorus
      Remember our grief,
O heart, when the rapturous season is o'er us
      Of blossom and leaf?
Their joy from the birds and the
streams let us borrow,
      O heart! let us sing,
The years are before us for weeping and sorrow . . .
      To-day it is spring!

SLUMBER
SONG FOR SUNALINI

In a Bengalee metre

WHERE the golden, glowing
Champak-buds are blowing,
By the swiftly-flowing streams,
Now, when day is dying,
There are fairies flying
Scattering a cloud of dreams.

Slumber-spirits winging
Thro' the forest singing,
Flutter hither bringing soon,
Baby-visions sheeny
For my Sunalini . . .
Hush thee, O my pretty moon!

Sweet, the saints shall bless thee . . .
Hush, mine arms caress thee,
Hush, my heart doth press thee, sleep,
Till the red dawn dances
Breaking thy soft trances,
Sleep, my Sunalini, sleep!

HYMN TO INDRA,
LORD OF RAIN

———————

Men's Voices:

O THOU, who rousest the voice of the thunder,
And biddest the storms to awake from their sleep,
Who breakest the strength of the mountains asunder,
And cleavest the manifold pride of the deep!
Thou, who with bountiful torrent and river
Dost nourish the heart of the forest and plain,
Withhold not Thy gifts O Omnipotent Giver!
          Hearken, O Lord of Rain!

Women's Voices:

O Thou, who wieldest Thy deathless dominion
O'er mutable legions of earth and the sky,
Who grantest the eagle the joy of her pinion,
And teachest the young of the *koel* to fly!
Thou who art mighty to succour and cherish,
Who savest from sorrow and shieldest from pain,
Withhold not Thy merciful love, or we perish,
                    Hearken, O Lord of Rain!

FAREWELL

BRIGHT shower of lambent butterflies,
Soft cloud of murmuring bees,
O fragile storm of sighing leaves
Adrift upon the breeze!

Wild birds with eager wings outspread
To seek an alien sky,
Sweet comrades of a lyric spring.
My little songs, good-bye !

THE
FLUTE-PLAYER
OF BRINDABAN

WHY didst thou play thy matchless flute
    'Neath the Kadamba tree,
And wound my idly dreaming heart
    With poignant melody,
So where thou goest I must go
    My flute-player with thee?

Still must I like a homeless bird
    Wander, forsaking all
The earthly loves and worldly lures
    That held my life in thrall,
'And follow, follow, answering
    Thy magical flute-call.

To Indra's golden-flowering groves
    Where streams immortal flow,
Or to sad Yama's silent Courts
    Engulfed in lampless woe,
Where'er thy subtle flute I hear
    Belovèd I must go!

No peril of the deep or height
    Shall daunt my wingèd foot;
No fear of time-unconquered space,
    Or light untravelled route,
Impede my heart that pants to drain
    The nectar of thy flute!

Krishna, the Divine Flute-player of Brindaban, who plays the tune of the infinite that lures every Hindu heart away from mortal cares and attachments.

THE
GARDEN VIGIL

In the deep silence of the garden-bowers
Only the stealthy zephyr glides and goes,
Rifling the secret of sirisha flowers,
And to the new-born hours
Bequeathes the subtle anguish of the rose.

Pain-weary and dream-worn I lie awake,
Counting like beads the blazing stars o'erhead;
Round me the wind-stirred champak branches shake
Blossoms that fall and break
In perfumed rain across my lonely bed.

Long ere the sun's first far-off beacons shine,
Or her prophetic clarions call afar,
The gorgeous planets wither and decline,
Save in its eastern shrine,
Unquenched, unchallenged, the proud morning star.

O glorious light of hope beyond all reach!
O lovely symbol and sweet sign of him
Whose voice I yearn to hear in tender speech
To comfort me or teach,
Before whose gaze thy golden fires grow dim!

I care not what brave splendours bloom or die
So thou dost burn in thine appointed place,
Supreme in the still dawn-uncoloured sky,
And daily grant that I
May in thy flame adore His hidden face.

THE PEARL

How long shall it suffice
      Merely to hoard in thine unequalled rays
    The bright sequestered colours of the sun,
O pearl above all price,
      And beautiful beyond all need of praise,
    World-coveted but yet possessed of none,
    Content in thy proud self-dominion?

Shall not some ultimate
      And unknown hour deliver thee, an attest
    Life's urgent and inviolable claim
To bind and consecrate
      The glory on some pure and bridal breast,
    Or set thee to enhance with flawless flame
    A new-born nation's coronal of fame?

Or wilt thou self-denied
      Forgo such sweet and sacramental ties
    As weld Love's delicate bonds of ecstasy,
And in a barren pride
      Of cold, unfruitful freedom that belies
    The inmost secret of fine liberty
    Return unblest into the primal sea?

KALI THE MOTHER

All Voices:

    O TERRIBLE and tender and divine!
    O mystic mother of all sacrifice,
    We deck the sombre altars of thy shrine
    With sacred basil leaves and saffron rice;
    All gifts of life and death we bring to thee,
        Uma Haimavati!

Maidens:

    We bring thee buds and berries from the wed!

Brides:

    We bring the rapture of our bridal prayer!

Mothers:

    And we the sweet travail of motherhood!

Widows:

    And we the bitter vigils of despair!

All Voices:

> All gladness and all grief we bring to thee,
> > *Ambika! Parvati!*

Artisans:

> We bring the lowly tribute of our toil!

Peasants:

> We bring our new-born goats and budded wheat!

Victors:

> And we the swords and symbols of our spoil!

Vanquished:

> And we the shame and sorrow of defeat!

All Voices:

> All triumph and all tears we bring to thee,
> > *Girija! Shambhavi!*

Scholars:

> We bring the secrets of our ancient arts.

Priests:

>   We bring the treasures of our ageless creeds.

Poets:

>   And we the subtle music of our hearts.

Patriots:

>   And we the sleepless worship of our deeds.

All Voices:

>   All glory and all grace we bring to thee,
>   *Kali! Maheshwari!* [1]

---

1   These are some of the many names of
Kali the Eternal Mother of Hindu worship.

THE
TIME OF ROSES

———————

LOVE, it is the time of roses!
In bright fields and garden closes
How they burgeon and unfold!
How they sweep o'er tombs and towers
In voluptuous crimson showers
And untrammelled tides of gold!

How they lure wild bees to capture
All the rich mellifluous rapture
Of their magical perfume,
And to passing winds surrender
All their frail and dazzling splendour
Rivalling your turban-plume!

How they cleave the air adorning
The high rivers of the morning
In a blithe, bejewelled fleet!
How they deck the moonlit grasses
In thick rainbow-tinted masses
Like a fair queen's bridal sheet!

Hide me in a shrine of roses,
Drown me in a wine of roses
Drawn from every fragrant grove!
Bind me on a pyre of roses,
Burn me in a fire of roses,
Crown me with the rose of Love!

CAPRICE

You held a wild flower in your fingertips,
Idly you pressed it to indifferent lips,
Idly you tore its crimson leaves apart . . .
Alas! it was my heart.

You held a wine-cup in your fingertips,
Lightly you raised it to indifferent lips,
Lightly you drank and flung away the bowl . . .
Alas! it was my soul.

DESTINY

IT chanced on the noon of an April day
A dragon-fly passed in its sunward play
And furled his flight for a passing hour
To drain the life of a passion-flower . . .
Who cares if a ruined blossom die,
O bright blue wandering dragon-fly?

Love came, with his ivory flute,
His pleading eye, and his winged foot:
"I am weary," he murmured; "O let me rest
In the sheltering joy of your fragrant breast."
At dawn he fled and he left no token . . .
Who cares if a woman's heart be broken?

ASHOKA BLOSSOM

IF a lovely maiden's foot
Treads on the Ashoka root,
Its glad branches sway and swell,
So our eastern legends tell,
Into gleaming flower,
Vivid clusters golden-red
To adorn her brow or bed
Or her marriage bower.

If your glowing foot be prest
O'er the secrets of my breast,
Love, my dreaming head would wake,
And its joyous fancies break
Into lyric bloom
To enchant the passing world
With melodious leaves unfurled
And their wild perfume.

ATONEMENT

DEEP in a lonely garden on the hill,
        Lulled by the low sea-tides,
A shadow set in shadows, soft and still,
        A wandering spirit glides,
    Smiting its pallid palms and making moan
    O let my Love atone!

Deep in a lonely garden on the hill
        Among the fallen leaves
A shadow lost in shadows, vague and chill,
        A wandering spirit grieves,
    Beating its pallid breast and making moan
    O let my Death atone!

SUMMER WOODS

O I AM tired of painted roofs and soft and silken
  floors,
And long for wind-blown canopies of crimson
  gulmohars!

O I am tired of strife and song and festivals and
  fame,
And long to fly where cassia-woods are breaking into
  flame.

Love, come with me where koels all from flowering
  glade and glen,
Far from the toil and weariness, the praise and
  prayers of men.
 O let us fling all care away, and lie alone and dream
'Neath tangled boughs of tamarind and molsari and
  neem!

And bind our brows with jasmine sprays and play on
   carven flutes,
To wake the slumbering serpent-kings among the
   banyan roots.

 And roam at fall of eventide along the river's brink,
And bathe in water-lily pools where golden panthers
   drink!

You and I together, Love, in the deep blossoming
   woods
Engirt with love-voiced silences and gleaming
   solitudes.

Companions of the lustrous dawn, gay comrades of
   the night,
Like Krishna and like Radhika, encompassed with
   delight.

JUNE SUNSET

HERE shall my heart find its haven of calm,
By rush-fringed rivers and rain-fed streams
That glimmer thro' meadows of lily and palm.
Here shall my soul find its true repose
Under a sunset sky of dreams
Diaphanous, amber and rose.
The air is aglow with the glint and whirl
Of swift wild wings in their homeward flight,
Sapphire, emerald, topaz, and pearl.
Afloat in the evening light.

A brown quail cries from the tamarisk bushes,
A bulbul calls from the cassia-plume,
And thro' the wet earth the gentian pushes
Her spikes of silvery bloom.

Where'er the foot of the bright shower passes
Fragrant and fresh delights unfold;
The wild fawns feed on the scented grasses,
Wild bees on the cactus-gold.

An ox-cart stumbles upon the rocks,
And a wistful music pursues the breeze
From a shepherd's pipe as he gathers his flocks
Under the pipal trees.
And a young Banjara driving her cattle
Lifts up her voice as she glitters by
In an ancient ballad of love and battle
Set to the beat of a mystic tune,
And the faint stars gleam in the eastern sky
To herald a rising moon.

AUTUMN SONG

LIKE a joy on the heart of a sorrow,
        The sunset hangs on a cloud;
A golden storm of glittering sheaves,
Of fair and frail and fluttering leaves,
        The wild wind blows in a cloud.

Hark to a voice that is calling
        To my heart in the voice of the wind:
My heart is weary and sad and alone,
For its dreams like the fluttering leaves have gone,
        And why should I stay behind?

HARVEST HYMN

Men's Voices

LORD of the lotus, lord of the harvest,
Bright and munificent lord of the morn!
Thine is the bounty that prospered our sowing,
Thine is the bounty that nurtured our corn.
We bring thee our songs and our garlands for tribute,
The gold of our fields and the gold of our fruit;
O giver of mellowing radiance, we hail thee,
We praise thee, O Surya, with cymbal and flute.

Lord of the rainbow, lord of the harvest,
Great and beneficent lord of the main!
Thine is the mercy that cherished our furrows,
Thine is the mercy that fostered our grain.
We bring thee our thanks and our garlands for tribute,
The wealth of our valleys, new-garnered and ripe;
O sender of rain and the dewfall, we hail thee,
We praise thee, Varuna, with cymbal and pipe.

Women's Voices

Queen of the gourd-flower, queen of the harvest,
Sweet and omnipotent mother, O Earth!
Thine is the plentiful bosom that feeds us,
Thine is the womb where our riches have birth.
We bring thee our love and our garlands for tribute,
With gifts of thy opulent giving we come;
O source of our manifold gladness, we hail thee,
We praise thee, O Prithvi, with cymbal and drum.

All Voices

Lord of the Universe, Lord of our being,
Father eternal, ineffable Om!
Thou art the Seed and the Scythe of our harvests,
Thou art our Hands and our Heart and our Home.
We bring thee our lives and our labours for tribute,
Grant us thy succour, thy counsel, thy care.
O Life of all life and all blessing, we hail thee,
We praise thee, O Bramha, with cymbal and prayer.

THE
MAGIC OF SPRING

———————

I BURIED my heart so deep, so deep,
Under a secret hill of pain,
And said: "O broken pitiful thing
Even the magic spring
Shall ne'er wake thee to life again,
Tho' March woods glimmer with opal rain
And passionate koels sing."

The kimshuks burst into dazzling flower,
The seemuls burgeoned in crimson pride,
The palm-groves shone with the oriole's wing,
The koels began to sing,
The soft clouds broke in a twinkling tide . . .
My heart leapt up in its grave and cried.
"Is it the spring, the spring?"

IN PRAISE OF
GULMOHUR BLOSSOMS

———————

WHAT can rival your lovely hue
O gorgeous boon of the spring?
The glimmering red of a bridal robe,
Rich red of a wild bird's wing?
Or the mystic blaze of the gem that burns
On the brow of a serpent-king?

What can rival the valiant joy
Of your dazzling, fugitive sheen?
The limpid clouds of the lustrous dawn
That colour the ocean's mien?
Or the blood that poured from a thousand breasts
To succour a Rajput queen?[2]

———————

2   Queen Padmini of Chitore, famous
in Indian history and song.

THE
CALL OF SPRING

To Padmaja and Lilamani

CHILDREN, my children, the spring wakes anew,
And calls through the dawn and the daytime
For flower-like and fleet-footed maidens like you,
To share in the joy of its play-time.

O'er hill-side and valley, through
garden and grove,
Such exquisite anthems are ringing
Where rapturous bulbul and maina and dove
Their carols of welcome are singing.

I know where the ivory lilies unfold
In brooklets half-hidden in sedges,
And the air is aglow with the blossoming gold
Of thickets and hollows and hedges.

I know where the dragon-flies glimmer and glide,
And the plumes of wild peacocks are gleaming,
Where the fox and the squirrel
and timid fawn hide
And the hawk and the heron lie dreaming.

The earth is ashine like a humming-bird's wing,
And the sky like a kingfisher's feather,
O come, let us go and play with the spring
Like glad-hearted children together.

A SONG IN SPRING

WILD bees that rifle the mango blossom,
Set free awhile from the love-god's string,
Wild birds that sway in the citron branches,
Drunk with the rich, red honey of spring,

Fireflies weaving aërial dances
In fragile rhythms of flickering gold,
What do you know in your blithe, brief season
Of dreams deferred and a heart grown old?

But the wise winds know, as they pause to slacken
The speed of their subtle, omniscient flight,
Divining the magic of unblown lilies,
Foretelling the stars of the unborn night.

They have followed the hurrying feet of pilgrims,
Tracking swift prayers to their utmost goals,
They have spied on Love's old and changeless secret,
And the changing sorrow of human souls.

They have tarried with Death in her parleying-places,
And issued the word of her high decree,
Their wings have winnowed the garnered sunlight,
Their lips have tasted the purple sea.

BIBLIOGRAPHY

TO MY FAIRY FANCIES,
  First published in 1905, *The Golden Threshold.*
LEILI,
  First published in 1905, *The Golden Threshold.*
IN THE FOREST,
  First published in 1905, *The Golden Threshold.*
IN A TIME OF FLOWERS,
  First published in 1912, *The Bird of Time*
  - Songs of Life, Death & the Spring.
NASTURTIUMS,
  First published in 1912, *The Bird of Time*
  - Songs of Life, Death & the Spring.
GOLDEN CASSIA,
  First published in 1912, *The Bird of Time*
  - Songs of Life, Death & the Spring.
CHAMPAK BLOSSOMS,
  First published in 1912, *The Bird of Time*
  - Songs of Life, Death & the Spring.

ECSTASY,

> First published in 1912, *The Bird of Time*
> *- Songs of Life, Death & the Spring.*

SLUMBER SONG FOR SUNALINI,

> First published in 1912, *The Bird of Time*
> *- Songs of Life, Death & the Spring.*

HYMN TO INDRA, LORD OF RAIN,

> FFirst published in 1912, *The Bird of Time*
> *- Songs of Life, Death & the Spring.*

FAREWELL,

> First published in 1912, *The Bird of Time*
> *- Songs of Life, Death & the Spring.*

THE FLUTE-PLAYER OF BRINDABAN,

> First published in 1917, *The Broken Wing*
> *- Songs of Love, Death & the Spring.*

THE GARDEN VIGIL,

> First published in 1917, *The Broken Wing*
> *- Songs of Love, Death & the Spring.*

THE PEARL,

> First published in 1917, *The Broken Wing*
> *- Songs of Love, Death & the Spring.*

KALI THE MOTHER,

> First published in 1917, *The Broken Wing*
> *- Songs of Love, Death & the Spring.*

THE TIME OF ROSES,
> First published in 1917, *The Broken Wing*
> *- Songs of Love, Death & the Spring.*

CAPRICE,
> First published in 1917, *The Broken Wing*
> *- Songs of Love, Death & the Spring.*

DESTINY,
> First published in 1917, *The Broken Wing*
> *- Songs of Love, Death & the Spring.*

ASHOKA BLOSSOM,
> First published in 1917, *The Broken Wing*
> *- Songs of Love, Death & the Spring.*

ATONEMENT,
> First published in 1917, *The Broken Wing*
> *- Songs of Love, Death & the Spring.*

SUMMER WOODS,
> First published in 1917, *The Broken Wing*
> *- Songs of Love, Death & the Spring.*

JUNE SUNSET,
> First published in 1917, *The Broken Wing*
> *- Songs of Love, Death & the Spring.*

AUTUMN SONG,
> First published in 1905, *The Golden Threshold.*

HARVEST HYMN,

First published in 1905, *The Golden Threshold.*

THE MAGIC OF SPRING,

First published in 1917, *The Broken Wing*
- Songs of Love, Death & the Spring.

IN PRAISE OF GULMOHUR BLOSSOMS,

First published in 1912, *The Bird of Time*
- Songs of Life, Death & the Spring.

THE CALL OF SPRING,

First published in 1917, *The Broken Wing*
- Songs of Love, Death & the Spring.

A SONG IN SPRING,

First published in 1912, *The Bird of Time*
- Songs of Life, Death & the Spring.